Working Paper Series
Congressional Budget Office
Washington, DC

Do We Know Why Earnings Fall with Job Displacement?

Abstract

After being displaced from their jobs, workers experience reduced earnings for many years and are at greater risks of other problems as well. The ills suffered by displaced workers motivated several recent expansions of government programs, including the unemployment insurance system, and have spurred calls for wage insurance that would provide longer-run earnings replacement. However, while the average size and the individual characteristics associated with the losses are relatively clear, the theory of displacement-induced earnings loss is scattered. Much of the policy discussion appears to interpret displacement-induced losses through the lens of specific human capital theory, in which skills are specific to jobs, locations, industries, or occupations, and that model has considerable empirical support. Assistance for displaced workers may improve well-being in that model since it insures workers against the risk that their consumption of goods and services might fall for idiosyncratic reasons and, as a consequence, allows workers to make more productive but higher-risk career choices. But there are other credible theories of costly job displacement that have different causal mechanisms, different interpretations and different policy implications. This paper reviews theories of costly job displacement and discusses their consistency with the available empirical evidence. We find that while specific human capital is important, we cannot rule out important roles for other theories.

Contents

I. Introduction

The recession of 2007-2009 displaced millions of workers in the United States and left them with the largest average earnings reductions since the Bureau of Labor Statistics (BLS) began the Displaced Worker Survey in 1984 (Bureau of Labor Statistics, 2014). Concern about the plight of displaced workers led to repeated expansions of the unemployment insurance (UI) program in the years after the onset of the recession in 2007 and, partly as a result, federal expenditures on UI benefits averaged roughly $100 billion annually (about 0.7% of GDP) from 2008 to 2012. Short-run UI payments account for most federal aid to displaced workers, but longer-term earnings replacement is available to some displaced workers through the Trade Adjustment Assistance (TAA) program. Several analysts have advocated that earnings insurance be extended to a much wider set of laid-off workers (Kletzer and Rosen, 2006; LaLonde, 2007).

The theory most commonly associated with the earnings losses of displaced workers is the specific human capital model of Gary Becker (1962) and Walter Oi (1962). In that model, job loss reduces earnings because job-specific human capital is lost with displacement or, more precisely, because demand for that particular type of human capital declines, making it less valuable. Similar reasoning has been applied to human capital that may be specific to workers' former locations, industries, or occupations – broader dimensions along which labor demand may fall. Workers in these models invest in human capital specific to their firms, occupations, or industries, and the loss in the value of those investments that accompanies displacement is largely due to bad luck. Because the loss is mostly due to bad luck, ex post transfers from people whose investments paid off to people whose investments did not pay off provide insurance to all and may encourage more investment in socially productive but privately risky specific human capital, as in Acemoglu and Shimer (2000). While the connection is rarely explicitly drawn, specific human capital theory appears to supply much of the logic behind efforts to assist displaced workers (e.g., von Wachter, 2010).

However, the literature includes other theories that may explain why workers' earnings tend to fall with displacement. Lazear (1979), for example, posits that wages rise with job tenure because firms defer some compensation and thereby require workers to build up *de facto* bonds with the firm. These bonds deter shirking and are paid back in the form of wages for high-tenure workers that are higher than their instantaneous marginal products. Displaced workers may be deprived of the repayment of some or all of their bonds. Similar effects are obtained in the model of Salop and Salop (1976) with neither specific human capital nor shirking. Firms in that model incur a fixed cost with each new worker and therefore firms lose money when workers leave before the firm recoups that expense. As a result, firms backload compensation to attract more stable workers. Earnings fall with displacement in both of those models, but the mechanisms differ significantly from that of specific human capital theory. Displacement may not be unexpected in those models and, even when it is a surprise, the economic notion of what is lost may be only weakly tied to the reduction in earnings as conventionally measured.

This paper reviews those and other theories of displaced workers' earnings losses and considers each theory's ability to explain the range of outcomes identified in the now-rich empirical literature. Section II reviews a range of theories and, for each theory, examines the causal mechanism behind costly displacement, whether losses vary by characteristics of workers, and whether the loss represents a social loss as well as a private loss to the worker. Section III confronts the various theories with the empirical experience of displaced workers. We note that each of the theories considered here was developed to explain a range of facts broader than the outcomes for displaced workers, and thus our focus on the theories' ability to explain the experience of displaced workers does not constitute an evaluation of the theories wider applicability. Section IV summarizes our findings and suggests some avenues for further research.

II. Theories of Costly Job Displacement

The idea that job loss is costly is almost as old as empirical labor economics, and has been well-established in the modern literature on displaced workers (Ruhm 1991; Jacobson, LaLonde, and Sullivan 1993; Couch and Placzek, 2010; von Wachter, Song, and Manchester, 2009).[1] The

---

[1] More recently, however, a few studies have called into question the notion that job loss itself leads to large and persistent earnings losses. See Fallick, Haltiwanger, and McEntarfer (2012); Flaaen, Shapiro, and Sorkin (2013); and Cooper (2013), whose findings suggest that presence or absence of displacement, at least as conventionally identified, is less important for earnings losses than the presence of an unemployment or nonemployment spell following separation.

earliest work on human capital earnings functions posited that a worker's earnings rose with education, with general labor market experience, and with the tenure on a specific job (Becker, 1962; Oi, 1962; Mincer, 1962). While it was not typically emphasized, an implication of those studies is that being forcibly deprived of job tenure would entail a loss in earnings. That finding was initially accompanied by the theory of firm-specific human capital but over time a variety of other interpretations arose, the most prominent of which are summarized in Table 1. This section lays out the basic architecture of those theories and points out some of their empirical implications.

Theories Based on Specific Human Capital

The earliest theories of costly job loss are based on the notion of specific human capital. The idea is that workers have a component of skill that is productive only at their current job. In the original formulations of Becker, Mincer and Oi, that specific skill develops over time, either through formal on-the-job training or through learning-by-doing on the job. Theorists have been vague about the character of the specific skills being developed because of the wide range of skills and knowledge that can be productive only in particular jobs. To take a few examples, knowledge of some specialized mathematics might be useful only in a missile plant; being able to operate a specialized lathe may be most useful at a particular machine shop; or a set of personal connections may be pertinent only at a particular law firm.

The fact that workers may be more productive at their current jobs than at any other, and that the magnitude of that wedge may change over time, spawned a modest theoretical challenge. In particular, there is no convincing theory of how those ex post rents are divided between firms and workers. The prevailing wisdom in the literature is that workers and firms split the investment returns, and, to the extent that there is an upfront training period in which productivity lags what it would be if no training took place, they may split the upfront costs as well. The joint nature of both the investments in and the returns to specific human capital creates an incentive for the worker and firm to preserve the employment relationship, leading to longer-tenured jobs than would exist in the absence of specific human capital.

The underlying cause of the earnings loss associated with displacement is easy to see in these models. Workers develop a stock of firm-specific skills whose rental price is tied to the demand conditions for that firm's product or services. If that firm fails or contracts, then the rental price for those skills falls, perhaps to zero, and the workers are left with only whatever general human capital they might have accumulated through education or work experience. The main implications of the specific human capital model are that job displacement reduces wages and earnings and that the magnitude of those earnings losses is tied to pre-displacement tenure. The most basic models of specific human capital predict that displacements of workers with minimal job tenure should not lead to significant earnings losses. Those workers have simply not had time to accumulate a sizeable stock of specific human capital that could then be devalued by the layoff. Instead, earnings losses should be concentrated in high-tenure displaced workers. What exactly it means to be "high tenure" is an empirical question, but the BLS, for example, bases many of its tabulations on outcomes for workers displaced from jobs they had held for at least three years. That type of restriction has been used in much of the academic work on job displacement as well (Jacobson, LaLonde, and Sullivan, 1993), but the choice of three years is somewhat arbitrary.

The original models of specific human capital were based on the notion on *firm* specificity, but from the start it was obvious that skills could also be specific to the type of work being done, the type of firm in which the work was performed, or on other dimensions of specificity, such as location. Those ideas later found expression in empirical work on occupations (Shaw, 1984), industries (Carrington 1993; Fallick, 1993; Neal, 1995), and locales (Howland and Peterson, 1988). At a mechanical level, there is little difference between these theories in how human capital comes to be specific. In any of those cases, workers' skills become specialized either through formal training or, likely more importantly, through the accretion of knowledge that comes with working in a field. There are differences among the versions of human capital theory, however, in how earnings are likely to vary with time at a particular employer. In particular, employers are less likely to "pay" —in the form of compensation that is above contemporaneous value marginal product—for learning that can be used at other employers. To do so invites workers to get training at an initial employer's expense and to then take that knowledge to a second, similar employer that is now willing to pay more because it does not have to recoup the costs of the training. These models do not imply that workers displaced from particular jobs will receive lower earnings if they are able to find reemployment in the same industries or occupations. However, theories based on specific human capital, along any

4

dimension, have a hard time explaining why some workers' earnings would *rise* with displacement.

We are not aware of any explicit theoretical analysis of the social costs of job displacement in the context of specific human capital models. The reduced earnings associated with loss of specific human capital upon displacement can have either social costs or purely private costs; the outcome depends on the nature of the events that reduced the value of that human capital. For example, suppose that an inexpensive new machine is developed that completely obviates the need for occupation A. In the standard calculus, this development is a social improvement because it increases overall productivity, though of course the workers in occupation A might be made worse off by their sudden obsolescence. As a second example, suppose that a newly formed industry cartel restricts supply and makes it necessary to displace some workers. This leads to a social cost as well a private cost since overall productivity is decreased. The key distinction here is whether the reduced value of the displaced worker's marginal product at the previous job is due to desirable changes in the underlying economic environment – for example, owing to technical change or changes in the terms of international trade – or whether the value is reduced by economic changes, such as cartelization, that an informed social planner would not approve.[2]

Theories Based on Job Matching

If specific human capital developed solely through work experience was the only source of earnings specificity, then how could some workers enjoy higher earnings in their next job after being displaced and losing their old firm-specific human capital?[3] One important answer to that

---

[2] A less conventional analysis of social efficiency might focus on workers' willingness – or lack thereof – to adapt to their straitened circumstances. Various socially efficient changes, such as labor-saving technical change, may reduce workers' productivity relative to what it was but still leave value marginal product above what it is at their next best alternatives. To fix ideas, suppose that a widget maker is paid $15 per hour on a long-term job and that their next-best alternative is $10 per hour. The long run value of an experienced widget-maker is then reduced by a change in widget-making technology so that their value marginal product is now $12 per hour. If the workers would accept a reduction in their wage to somewhere between $12 and $10, then the socially efficient matches between worker and firm would continue (McLaughlin, 1991). But if workers or the employer are unwilling to accept such a reduction from their current employer, then displacements and attendant earnings loss may occur even though it would be socially efficient for the worker and firm to stay together. The literature explores various reasons why that may occur (Hall and Lazear 1984; Bewley 1999).

[3] A more general challenge to specific human capital theory is that people voluntarily change jobs and that those job changes often lead to higher, not lower, wages. Indeed, Topel and Ward (1991) found that about one-third of the total earnings growth of young men could be attributed to earnings growth after (mostly voluntary) job changes.

question has been the job matching model of Jovanovic (1979a). In that model, there is a productivity component that is specific to particular matches of workers and firms. That component could be a particular skill, a personality trait, or an ability to tolerate particular conditions, that is more valuable at some firms than at others. Unlike in conventional specific human capital theory, however, that component is fixed and does not change over the course of a worker's stint with a particular employer. If information about the quality of a job match is revealed only through experience on the job — say, because employers learn over time whether a new worker is good at the tasks they need performed, or because workers learn about their preferences for various non-wage workplace attributes — then a job matching model can mimic many of the features of the specific human capital model. In particular, workers are most likely to quit a job within the first few years as they learn whether or not they are good matches with their jobs, and earnings rise with tenure because the only matches that survive are those for which good news about the match has accumulated and, as a result of the good news, earnings rise.

The implications of job matching theory for the experience of displaced workers are similar to those of specific human capital theory. Earnings fall with displacement because the workers were, on average, in high-quality matches that, as of the date of their displacement, paid correspondingly well. Being deprived of that high-quality match is costly because the worker will be forced to begin the job-matching process anew and test out another job that will typically be of lower match quality.[4] Losses will likely be highest for the most experienced workers, as they have had the longest time to sort themselves into a high-quality match prior to their displacement. The ability of job matching to explain the tenure profile of earnings loss is less than obvious, however. Suppose that workers receive a steady or predictable flow of draws from a fixed job match distribution and that they choose to work at the highest match received to date. Then, as Topel (1991) points out, a worker's years of experience is a sufficient statistic for the highest draw received and, in contrast, job tenure only indicates the order in which the best offer was received. However, the value of specific human capital should be highest in high-quality matches, as deliberate investments in human capital, such as training, are more likely to pay off

---

[4] Krolikowski (2014) demonstrates how such a model can reproduce many of the empirical features of displacement.

in a durable match (Jovanovic, 1979b). Thus, the two theories are properly viewed as complements as well as substitutes.

An additional implication of matching theory, however, is that some of those forced to search for a new position will find a *better* match than the one from which they were displaced, resulting in higher post-displacement earnings. That cannot happen in the most straightforward models of specific human capital. As with specific human capital, job matching theory can be extended, subject to some modifications, to specialization along the dimensions of industry, occupation, or locale. As Neal (1999) shows, young workers change occupations and industries more often than older workers in a way consistent with the view that workers search while young for a good occupation or industry match. Being displaced in one's youth is less costly, from this perspective, because younger workers are less likely to have sorted themselves into their highest and best use, and because being displaced from a not-so-good match is less costly to the worker in the long-run.

Some commonalities and differences between models based on firm-specificity

Education may also play an important role in both job matching and specific human capital theories.[5] There are clearly some skills that can be accumulated through education that will find productive expression only with a handful of employers, perhaps because the relevant industry is dominated by a few firms. If demand from those employers should decrease, workers with these skills would likely see a substantial reduction in the demand for their services. That would have little to do, however, with human capital that was accumulated while working for those particular firms. Rather, the loss would simply be associated with specialization that occurred within the education system. As one example, Embry-Riddle Aeronautical University graduates the country's largest class of aerospace engineers, most of whom are likely to find employment with the handful of airplane manufacturing firms in the United States. While aerospace engineering is an extreme case in that one company, Boeing, dominates that field to an unusual extent, there are many educational fields in which the successful use of the acquired

---

[5] There is some intrinsic ambiguity about whether education targeted toward employment with a specific employer should be viewed as a match or specific human capital. We focus here on the match interpretation, but in some cases, particularly where a firm pays for education in return for the promise of return employment, the conventional specific human capital interpretation is perhaps more valid.

skills is likely limited to a small set of prospective employers or by a larger set of employers, perhaps in the same industry, whose labor demand is highly correlated.

The implications of job matching theory for how to interpret the costs of job displacement have not, to our knowledge, been formally worked out. However, it would seem that much of the same logic applies here as applied to specific human capital: Workers are typically made worse off by a displacement, and the social costs hinge on the nature of the events that shifted in labor demand away from the workers' current employers. There is one important difference, however. Specific human capital is acquired over time and is the product of decisions by workers on which jobs to hold and by employers on which types of training to provide. Those choices entail real opportunity costs in that other jobs were not pursued and in that other types of training were not provided. Thus, job displacement devalues human capital that could have been developed along other lines. That stands in contrast to the skills and preferences embodied in job matching models, in which the attributes exist prior to the start of the employment relationship.

Some problems with models based on firm-specificity

A problem with theories both of *firm*-specific human capital and of *firm*-specific matching is that relatively few skills – outside of personal connections to employees and customers – are completely specific to a single firm, as opposed to a broader occupation or industry. Lazear (2009) addresses that problem by positing that a worker's productivity at any particular firm is a function of the combination of an underlying set of skills – say, writing, computer programming, and accounting. Any given skill is valued at a range of firms, so that no skill is completely firm-specific, but firms vary in the weights that their production function puts on various skills. If a worker knew that he or she would stay at a firm forever, that worker would accumulate skills along the dimensions most valued by that firm. But that is a risky strategy if the firm values an idiosyncratic combination of skills – say, being both a doctor and a statistician – because if the firm fails there is not likely to be a firm that values that combination of skills in precisely the same way. A worker laid off from such a firm is likely to sustain a significant loss in earnings capacity. In contrast, a worker laid off from a firm with less idiosyncratic skill needs is likely to experience small or negligible costs from displacement.

A feature of the model in Lazear (2009) is that workers face a choice in whether to invest in combinations of skills in thinly-traded portions of the skill distribution – that is, those with few employers desiring those particular combinations of skills – or, alternatively, to invest in skill combinations that are more thickly traded. In equilibrium, investments in thinly-traded skill combinations have higher expected returns, but they also entail more risk than investments in thickly-traded skill combinations, as in Murphy (1986). The focus on the riskiness of specific human capital investment, and the expected premiums that accrue to workers that take on that risk, brings up an interesting issue of interpretation of earnings losses. In a model in which all workers invest in specific human capital with whatever firms they start with, the market for those skills is equally thick, and there is no variability in layoff risk. Workers start their careers on the same wage trajectory and continue until some of them are laid off, at which point those laid-off workers sustain a significant reduction in their earnings capacity. In that case, the lifetime earnings of displaced workers are less than those of the non-displaced for no reason other than luck. However, in a version of the model in which firms vary in their propensity to lay off workers or in which skills vary in the thickness of their markets, the workers who would sustain the biggest drop in earnings upon layoff ex post are presumably compensated for that risk ex ante in the form of higher pay. That theory is supported by the findings of Topel (1984) and others who find that workers with high risk of layoffs are paid more than similar workers with low layoff risk.

Those observations suggest that the benefits provided to displaced workers by UI and other programs may be disproportionately directed to workers that received some ex ante compensation for the risk of displacement. As an example, a bidding war between Microsoft and a software startup for the same young programmer may force the startup to make a higher bid to compensate the programmer for the higher risk of being laid off. Absent UI, those workers would have received higher pay ex ante, and those laid off from high-risk jobs that were held for longer than expected may not have lower lifetime income than those *not* laid off from jobs with low risks. The presence of UI, however, likely reduces the compensating differential that accrues to high-risk jobs. Topel (1984), for example, finds that more generous UI benefits lead workers to require less ex ante compensation to bear displacement risk. In the extreme version of a UI program that provided complete layoff insurance, making workers indifferent to whether they were laid off or not, the compensating differential for displacement risk would be zero.

Theories of Backloaded Compensation

The development of models of moral hazard and adverse selection in the 1970s gave rise to alternative theories that explain why workers' earnings might be tied to their specific employers. Spence (1973) reasoned that education could be viewed as a sorting mechanism that identified the subset of workers that could complete a college degree and, by extension, tasks that employers valued as well. Salop and Salop (1976) applied those ideas to the same set of facts that motivated specific human capital and job matching theory: High tenure workers had higher pay and were less likely to quit. In one formulation of that model, employers must pay some training costs for any newly hired worker and therefore have an incentive to attract workers who are unlikely to quit and thereby deprive the firm of a return on its investment. If workers vary in their intrinsic likelihood of quitting, then firms may offer wage-tenure profiles that are steeper than actual worker productivity. By doing so, firms can be viewed as requiring that workers post an upfront bond, in the form of foregone earnings, that is then repaid with above-productivity wages in later periods. If firms with high training costs use such tilted profiles while others do not, then the use of such profiles can efficiently sort high-mobility workers to those employers for whom that mobility is the least costly. Tilted age-earnings profiles may also help firms select workers with other desirable attributes, such as patience or the ability to work in teams.

A similar mechanism is behind the agency models of Lazear (1979, 1981). In those models, employers are concerned about moral hazard on the part of their workers in the form of theft, negligence, or any of a number of other difficult-to-monitor forms of shirking.[6] If firms are forced to pay all workers something close to their point-in-time marginal products, then workers, absent some other mechanism, will face little incentive to avoid shirking because the availability of similar jobs means that getting caught entails little punishment. Lazear points out that tilted wage-tenure profiles that generate an implicit bond provide an incentive for workers to avoid shirking, as the threat of being fired carries a real penalty – the loss of their bonds. Lazear (1979) used that reasoning to explain the existence of mandatory retirement policies, as firms that pay workers more than their marginal product in the latter years of their career will not want workers to hang on too long and potentially more than recoup the present value of the bond they

---

[6] See Dickens, Katz, Lang, and Summers (1989) for a discussion of the prevalence of employee crime and its implications for employer compensation policies.

implicitly paid in their earlier years of employment.[7] While designed for other purposes, the theory provides a novel perspective on the earnings losses of displaced workers.

A distinctive feature of that class of agency models is that while experienced workers may be paid more at their current jobs than they would be elsewhere, they are in fact no more productive at their current jobs than they would be elsewhere. Put differently, there is no direct loss in economy-wide production from moving workers from long-term jobs to jobs that they must start afresh. Workers will lose an amount that depends upon where they are in the process of recouping their bonds, but that does not result in an economic loss to society. Another distinctive feature of these models is that the interpretation of the loss varies with how long workers have been with a firm. Employment duration is non-stochastic in the original formulations of both models, but in fact there is always some uncertainty about how long any employment relationship will last. While the precise implications of randomly timed dissolutions have not (to our knowledge) been worked out in the literature, one possible solution would be that the time-paths of earnings are structured so as to, on average, leave workers being paid back their bonds with interest.[8] That means that workers whose employment is terminated before the expected end date will get back, on average, less than the value of the bonds that they implicitly paid.

In Figure 1 that loss starts at zero in the first period of employment and rises until the date t', at which point the worker's pay begins to exceed their value marginal product (VMP). The implicit bond is fully paid in at that point and it is at that point when the cost of displacement is maximized. Thereafter, compensation includes a component that is interpreted as the gradual payback of that bond and the cost of displacement decreases as the remaining implicit bond shrinks. At date T, when the job was forecast to come to an end, there is no loss to workers vis-à-vis their initial expectations, even though workers displaced upon that date will be quite

---

[7] Some theorists (for example, Shapiro and Stiglitz, 1984) posited that the wage effects of moral hazard were more likely to show up as an elevated equilibrium wage at which there was not full employment. In essence, the equilibrium existence of an army of unemployed kept the employed feeling lucky to have jobs and therefore unlikely to engage in malfeasance. Murphy and Topel (1990) argued on theoretical grounds that firms using implicit bonds will be more profitable than those paying efficiency wages a la Shapiro and Stiglitz, and therefore that firms using implicit bonds will tend to prevail in inter-firm competition.

[8] In the original Lazear (1979) model, the date of termination is nonstochastically set to be the date at which the opportunity cost of not working rises above the worker's value marginal product.

disappointed if they have to start back at lower salaries.

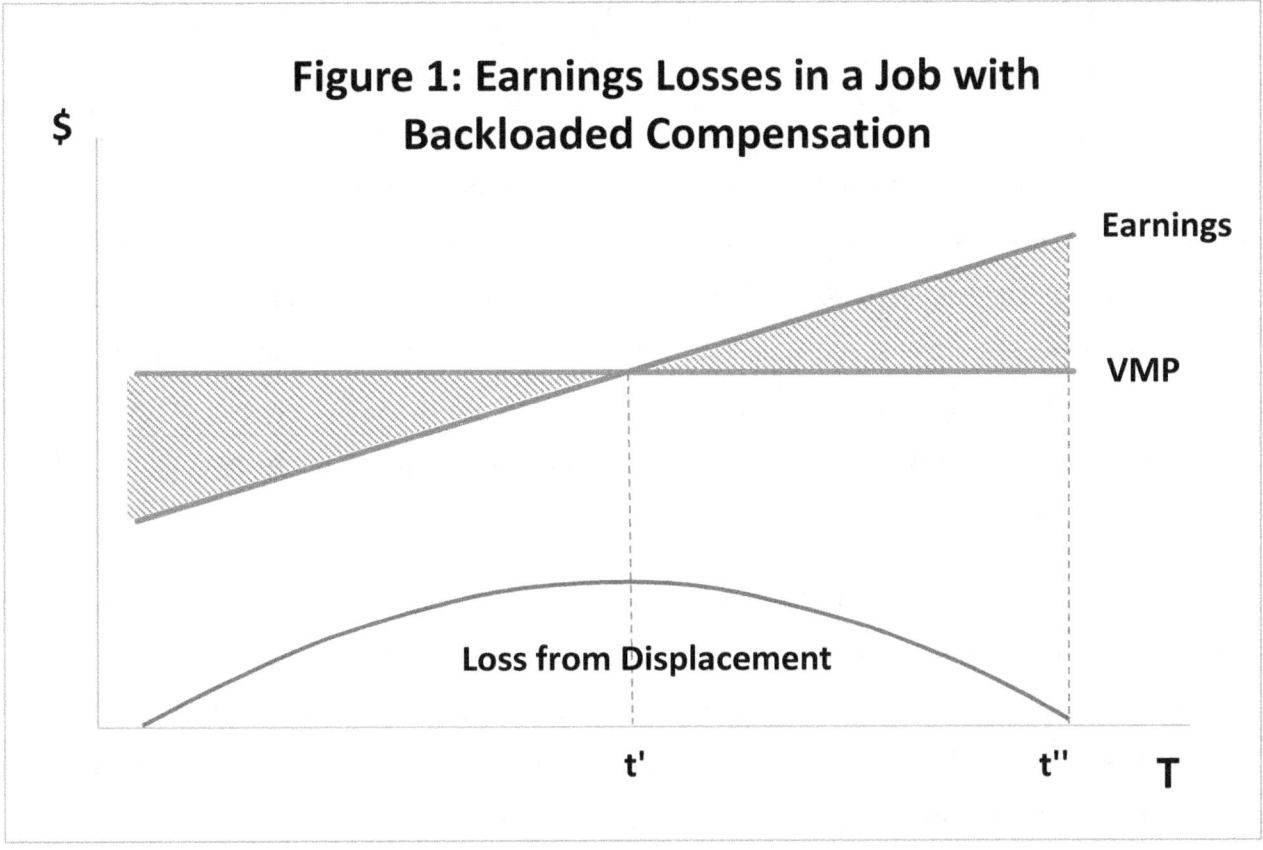

Figure 1: Earnings Losses in a Job with Backloaded Compensation

There are, then, two notions in these models of what might be lost in displacement. The first notion of cost is the private decrement in earnings that a displaced worker might experience as a result of being laid off. That decrement is typically measured as the difference between the worker's earnings at displacement and the worker's earnings after displacement. That decrement can be measured at a single point in time, at a series of points in time, or, as in Davis and von Wachter (2011), as a cumulative decrement over the worker's remaining career. As long as the gap between compensation and value marginal product continues to grow with job tenure, the loss in earnings upon reemployment after displacement is likely to increase steadily with tenure under any of these measures, and the highest tenure workers will experience the largest losses. A second notion of what is lost in displacement is the cumulative value of a worker's implicit bond at time of displacement. That would correspond to a measure of how damaged a worker ultimately was relative to expectations at the time he or she took the job. While the highest-tenure workers' contemporaneous earnings fall the most, they are not the most damaged by

12

having taken the jobs from which they were ultimately displaced. Workers would willingly take jobs from which they expected to be displaced at date t'', for example – indeed, in the original model, mandatory retirement is functionally equivalent to a job displacement. And workers would happily accept jobs from which they expected to be displaced at a still later date, because at that later date of displacement they will have received back, in the form of extra pay, *more* than they implicitly paid in during their first years of employment. In contrast, that second measure of displacement cost peaks at date t' in Figure 1, the date at which pay begins to exceed VMP. Thus, in an important sense, it is "mid-career," or, better yet, "mid-tenure" workers that are the most disadvantaged by a displacement in that setup. Workers at either end of the expected tenure range are, in contrast, not seriously disadvantaged over their careers by having taken the job from which they were displaced,

Theories of backloaded compensation, as well as human capital and matching theories, share the property that the rising wage (tenure or experience) profiles that make displacement costly are tied to workers' productivity or costs to the firm. It is assumed that the workers themselves are interested in maximizing the discounted stream of utility or, in simplified models, earnings. Some survey and experimental evidence, however, suggests that workers do not seek to maximize the present discounted value of earnings. In particular, workers may *prefer* rising earnings profiles – both within and across jobs – even when those earnings profiles offer less net present value than profiles that do not rise as rapidly over time (Loewenstein and Sicherman, 1991; Loewenstein and Prelec, 1993). There are a variety of ways to modify the standard intertemporal choice model to account for these preferences – for example, by assuming a low or negative discount rate or by assuming that workers view rising earnings profiles as a way to regulate their own savings behavior (much like some workers deliberately have too much income tax withheld from their paychecks).[9]

The interpretation of displacement-induced earnings losses in that case is similar to that of the class of models in which compensation is backloaded for reasons related to moral hazard (a

---

[9] There are obviously theoretical challenges to that interpretation of rising wage profiles – the main one being that there are several disadvantages to employees of having their employers serve as a savings bank. Doing so, for example, exposes employees to the prospect of being opportunistically fired by an employer that does not wish to repay the "savings" the employee accumulated and ties the repayment of the "savings" to the continued prosperity of the firm. Still, much of the recent economics and psychology literature suggests that consumers, under some circumstances, behave in ways at odds with conventional economic maximization.

la Lazear) or adverse selection (a la Salop and Salop). That is, any backloaded compensation scheme would seem to depend upon the expectations of employee and employer about the likely durability of the employment relationship. In that environment, employees who leave while the "bond" is still being paid in will have low contemporaneous changes in earnings, while at the same time they would be most damaged from a career perspective, as in Figure 1. In contrast, the long-time workers who are highly paid may experience large contemporaneous earnings losses even though they have stayed long enough to more than recoup any earlier periods of low pay. Thus, there is a substantial wedge between the economic loss incurred by displaced workers – defined as the gap between the discounted value they ultimately got from a job and the discounted value they expected upon accession – and the loss as conventionally estimated in most studies of displaced workers' earnings losses.

The loss of implicit bonds in displacement also raises issues of social costs. Given that the general feature of American employment law is employment at will, employers cannot guarantee that employees who pay in a bond will be allowed to stay around long enough to recoup.[10] That of course means that some employers may make such promises implicitly and then, either by plan or not, renege on those promises. That confiscation of an implicit bond generates a private transfer from the employee to the employer. But if the very existence of such contracts, which may be welfare-improving, relies on employers' collective reputations to make good on the contracts except under extreme fiscal distress, then layoffs by one employer may raise costs for other employers because it makes their promises to repay employees' bonds less credible, as in Klein, Crawford and Alchian (1978).

Rents

When a firm or industry is particularly profitable, those profits may be shared with workers in the form of pay higher than marginal product.[11] Pay may also exceed workers' marginal product at employers that are heavily regulated, unionized, or particularly profitable (Hildreth and Oswald, 1997). These rents, as opposed to the ex post quasi-rents implied by, say, human

---

[10] There is a longstanding trend, of course, towards the erosion of the employment-at-will doctrine (Krueger, 1991). Autor, Donohue and Schwab (2006) argue that the implied-contract exception to the employment-at-will doctrine, adopted by some states, has substantially reduced employment rates. That effect may in turn be due to firms' reduced willingness to finance specific human capital formation due to the greater financial risk imposed by the implied contract exception.

[11] See, for example, Blanchflower, Oswald, and Sanfey (1996).

capital theory, are not a return on an investment that is embodied in the worker; nor, as in agency theories, do they reflect an incentive mechanism. When market conditions turn against these firms or sectors and workers lose their jobs, the rents are likely lost to those workers. Although not models of rents, efficiency wage theories, as in Shapiro and Stiglitz (1984), also conclude that some workers are paid more than they would be were their current jobs to be eliminated, with similar implications for the workers.

It is useful to think of there being two versions of these types of models. In the first type, all employers pay rents or efficiency wages. Those workers with the rent-paying jobs are lucky, while those left out are unemployed. Displacement is costly in that setup because laid-off workers are unemployed until they accede to a second rent-paying job. In the second type of model, some employers pay rents or efficiency wages and others do not. Displacement from a rent-paying employer is again costly while displacement from a non-rent-paying employer is not. The average costliness of displacement would then depend upon the relative incidence of displacement from the two sorts of jobs. Note that there is no direct mechanism in either version that would lead the earnings loss associated with displacement to be correlated with job tenure.[12] Also worth noting is that in rent models, workers with the largest contemporaneous losses – that is, the largest declines in earnings upon displacement – were the luckiest ex ante.

There is no mechanism in those models whereby one firm's layoffs harm other firms or their workers. Thus, the earnings losses in those models are purely private. There also appears to be no efficiency rationale for displaced worker assistance, either, as the presence of insurance does not induce workers to take jobs that are riskier but also more productive, as in the Acemoglu and Shimer (2000) model.

Theories Based on Revelation of Information

Another set of theories of costly job displacement is based on the idea that employers have private knowledge about their workers' attributes, a realistic assumption for most occupations. A job displacement may then reveal to future employers something unfavorable about the displaced worker, something that only someone with day-to-day experience with the employee would

---

[12] Employees may be slower to quit high-rent jobs, however, which could lead to an empirical correlation between tenure and costs of job loss.

know. Prospective employers may conclude that the laid-off worker's marginal product at his prior firm was lower than that of the average worker with the same observable characteristics at the same firm. In that environment, being displaced is likely to lower a future employer's estimate of a worker's productivity, much like being dismissed for cause. Indeed, given the reticence of some former employers to publicize the fact that they may have dismissed a former employee for cause, prospective employers may lump all employees with dismissals on their application as being, probabilistically, a weighted average of those who were fired and those who were laid off.[13]

The widely cited "lemons" model of Gibbons and Katz (1991) is one application of those ideas. In that model, firms are not selective in whom they lay off when they close plants; all workers, good or bad, are let go. In contrast, employers are selective about who they let go in partial layoffs, tending to let go workers with the lowest ratio of productivity to earnings or labor cost. Knowing that, prospective new employers infer that workers displaced in a partial layoff event are less productive than those displaced in full plant closings and are willing to employ those displaced in partial layoffs only at wage rates lower than they had been receiving previously. In contrast, prospective employers draw no inference about a worker's quality when he or she is displaced in a plant closing, as in those cases the former employer was not selective as to whom it let go. Subsequent research has not consistently found that those displaced in partial layoffs lose more in earnings than those displaced in plant closings, so the mechanics of the Gibbons and Katz setup may be questioned. Nevertheless, the basic idea – that current employers have some private information about their workers' productivity – has survived.[14]

Even if one accepts that a worker's displacement is a bad signal to prospective employers, there are reasons to doubt the importance of a sharp dichotomy between plant closing and layoffs by continuing plants. Firms rarely move immediately from a state of either growing or stable employment growth to a state of decline or closure (Troske 1996) – thus, workers often have signals well-before their displacement that their employer is not doing well. As firms start to fail, workers who are the least attached to the firm, and whose pay is least elevated relative to their

---

[13] There is surprisingly little known about the frequency with which workers are fired or the wage effects of being fired, largely because all government surveys of which we are aware make no effective effort to distinguish between dismissal with and without cause.

[14] See, for example, Kahn (2013) and Michaud (2014).

next-best alternative, are those most likely to leave *before* the firm actually lays any one off or fails altogether. In contrast, those workers with poor outside opportunities relative to their current pay may stick with the firm until it completely shutters its operations. Some of the difference between workers' current salaries and their outside opportunities may come from the accumulation of firm-specific human capital, but it may also be that some workers are simply paid more at their current jobs than is justified by their productivity at that or any other job. Again, extreme cases of overpaid workers are likely to be fired or have their salary cut, but moderately overpaid workers may persist in the presence of firing costs or firms' reluctance to cut nominal salaries. From that perspective, it is no longer clear that workers let go in plant closures are not selected on quality or on the ratio of or difference between their pay and their productivity. Rather, the least overpaid workers may find outside opportunities quite palatable and leave early in the firm's decline, while those who are the most overpaid will attempt to stay around until they have no choice, with only the latter group being classified as being displaced.

Oyer and Schaefer (2000) argue that the high costs of an explicit firing – either due to concerns about litigation or due to managers' reluctance to take on the unpleasant task of firing a worker – may motivate firms to retain somewhat overpaid employees for a time. In their model, firms delay firing marginally overpaid workers until the firms both a) have a collection of such workers that they would like to fire, and b) experience a downturn in demand. When that happens, the firms "lay off" their collection of overpaid workers in a way that is less likely to directly insult workers, and therefore both less likely to lead to litigation and less stressful for the firing manager.[15] This reasoning suggests that a portion of the wage loss associated with displacement – either via layoff or through plant closure – could be interpreted as an implicit statement by the prior employer that the worker was a sub-par performer and was overpaid relative to their productivity.[16]

The interpretation of earnings losses is obviously quite different in that type of model than in, say, the standard specific human capital model. Earnings losses occur in the Oyer and

---

[15] That process is similar to theories of "reallocation timing," as in Davis' (1987).

[16] The amount of information revealed in a layoff may well have changed over time. The erosion of the employment-at-will doctrine in American employment law and the evolution of anti-discrimination law have likely had the effect of making it more expensive for firms for dismiss workers for cause (Krueger, 1991).

Schaefer model because displaced workers were previously "paid too much" relative to their productivities. That is clearly a private cost to the laid-off worker, but there are offsetting gains for the employer. Thus, the social costs are not obviously gauged or even signed, and depend upon whether the displaced workers are less productive at their subsequent jobs than they were at their previous jobs. It is even possible that some such displacements entail a social gain in the sense that workers are forced to relocate to jobs at which they are more productive, even though they are paid less.

Those considerations also raise important questions about how to define a displaced worker empirically. Conventional empirical work typically relies on one of two methods:

a) Survey workers directly as to whether they were displaced (as in the Displaced Worker Survey), or

b) Impute displacement based on a worker separating from an employer that concurrently either closed or reduced employment substantially (as in most analyses of administrative data).

Either of those approaches may miss workers who voluntarily leave a firm in decline before the displacements actually occur, and omitting those workers from consideration may be potentially misleading.[17] Indeed, workers who leave declining firms in the quarters prior to layoffs – and who would not be generally classified as having been displaced but are likely reacting to the same phenomena as workers who are eventually let go– appear to have higher earnings at the initial firm, higher earnings at subsequent employers, and much smaller reductions in earnings associated with leaving the failing firms (Bowlus and Vilhuber 2002; Schwerdt 2011). That suggests that those workers who stay with an employer with declining fortunes until it actually lays workers off may be an unrepresentative sample of the employer's pre-decline workforce and, more particularly, may be the subset of workers who have the most to lose by being forced into new work. The combination of apparent reluctance to leave a sinking ship and large earnings losses could merely reflect those workers' particularly high levels of specific human capital; but, as noted earlier, it could also be that those workers are aware that they are over-placed or

---

[17] That point is related to, but distinct from, the oft-observed decline in displaced workers' earnings prior to displacement.

overpaid in their current positions and are appropriately concerned about their ability to find comparably lucrative work.

Intra-household Reallocation

Most models of earnings losses of displaced workers focus on individual workers. But most displaced workers live in households with others, often with spouses, so it is natural to view displacement's effects in the context of the household budgeting and utility maximization. The most basic models of intra-household consumption and risk sharing suggest that the displacement of one household member is likely to increase the work hours of other household members. That may occur through both a household income effect – the household has less money and so other household members' leisure falls if it is a normal good – and through a substitution effect, whereby the household shifts collective hours worked towards those whose earnings capacity has not been diminished through displacement. There has long been recognition of an "added worker effect," which occurs when a spouse temporarily enters the labor market to cover some of the income lost when a spouse was displaced (Lundberg, 1985). If there is some persistence in decisions about intra-household allocation of time, then the added worker's participation may also be longstanding. In that case, a displaced worker's earnings may not recover, as the increased spousal income reduces the labor supply of the displaced worker or causes the worker to select a less onerous, lower paying job.

Such a response alters the interpretation of displacement-induced earnings losses. To take an extreme case, in a one-earner household where the two spouses' earnings capacities are equivalent and the two spouses' leisure or household labor are perfect substitutes, then there would be little loss in utility from the displacement, despite a large and persistent reduction in the displaced worker's earnings. In the opposite case, however, it would be costly for the spouses to switch work roles, and the loss in earnings of the displaced worker would be a useful guide to the household's total losses.

The extent to which households divide roles is of course affected by the risk of displacement and the extent of social insurance. A family whose sole earner is a construction worker at significant risk for layoff and who lives in a state with low UI benefits runs a significant financial risk. That risk can be alleviated if the other spouse works or at least develops a readily marketable skill that could be called into use in the event of spousal displacement. In that view, the incidence of displacement in the economy – and in specific occupations and industries – affect inter-household decisions on the accumulation of human capital and work experience. The opposite is also true: Households that have committed themselves to living off the earnings of a single member would suffer more in the event of that person's displacement, and therefore such sole earners have incentives to shy away from jobs and careers in which the incidence of displacement is high.

Access to social insurance can mitigate those considerations. Short-run insurance, such as the 26 weeks typically available through UI programs, reduces some of the risk of displacement in the short run, but does little to insure against long-term losses in earnings capacity because of displacement. Longer-term earnings insurance, of the sort advocated by LaLonde (2007), Kletzer and Rosen (2006), and others, provides more of that sort of insurance. Both short-run and long-run insurance protect workers against the loss of earnings because of displacement, perhaps inducing additional efficient risk taking as in Acemoglu and Shimer (2000) as well as possibly reducing work incentives. But the availability of those benefits also reduces the value of income insurance that would, in some cases, be provided by spouses and other family members.

Health-Related Theories

Another view of displacement-induced earnings losses is that displaced workers are scarred by the experience. That is, a worker's *general* human capital is impaired by the loss of a specific job. While we are unaware of any direct evidence on that score, it seems unlikely to us that displaced workers quickly lose general skills such as how to type, speak French, or apply rules of accounting. In contrast, displacement may well adversely affect health, as well as confidence, optimism, and other personality attributes associated with earnings success. More traditionally a subject for research by psychologists, there is a short but interesting literature within economics on the role of confidence, optimism, and health in economic outcomes.[18] To our knowledge,

---

[18] For example, in their study of self-confidence and motivation, Benabou and Tirole (2002) identify three benefits to having a good as opposed to an accurate view of one's abilities: consumption value (that is, thinking well of oneself feels good), signaling value (that is, thinking well of oneself helps convince others to take helpful actions), and a motivational value (thinking well of oneself improves one's willpower or, equivalently, decreases the cost of effort). Benabou and Tirole model self-confidence as a dynamic game played by different temporal versions of oneself, as in Laibson's (1997) hyperbolic discounting model. There can be both high and low self-confidence equilibria in the model and while "too much" overconfidence can be counterproductive, a limited amount of it is conducive to higher productivity. Bad luck, such as a displacement, can bump a person from a highly-productive

however, there has been no explicit theoretical development of the role of health in the earnings losses of displaced workers.

III. A Review of the Empirical Evidence

There are many studies of earnings and employment outcomes for displaced workers. In this section we review the findings of that literature with the goal of identifying empirical regularities that provide evidence for or against various theories of earnings losses from job displacement. We organize our discussion on a result-by-result basis and, after reviewing each result, outline what we perceive to be its implications for the relevance of competing theories. In particular, our review provides support for the following empirical regularities:

- Earnings losses are persistent,
- The range of earnings changes is wide,
- Earnings losses increase with "degree" of displacement,
- Earnings losses vary by amount of schooling and training,
- Earnings losses depend on macroeconomic conditions,
- Earnings losses are due in part to reduced rates of employment,
- Earnings losses vary by degree of employer distress,
- Earnings losses vary by sex, age and race, and
- Displacement harms health, particularly mental health.

We have focused on what we perceive to be the most salient empirical regularities and on a (surely incomplete) selection of the papers that document them.

Earnings Losses are Persistent

The earnings of displaced workers are reduced, on average, for many years after the displacement occurs (Ruhm 1991; Jacobson LaLonde and Sullivan 1993; Schoeni and Dardia 1996; von Wachter, Song, and Manchester 2009; von Wachter, Handwerker, and Hildreth 2009; Couch and Placzek 2010; Davis and von Wachter 2011). The size of the estimated earnings loss over time depends upon the population and time frame studied, and upon the way in which displacements are identified. Measurements of earnings losses are also sensitive to how analysts

---

and confident state of mind into a less-productive and unconfident state of mind. That lack of confidence can lead to lower earnings, potentially for a long period.

characterize the worker's "non-displacement earnings," that is, what the worker would have earned absent the displacement, which is obviously not observed. Among the sources of such counterfactual information have been extrapolations from the worker's pre-displacement wage trajectory and the experience of similar workers – sometimes from the same employer – who were not displaced, at least not contemporaneously. A common theme, however, is that displaced workers' earnings are reduced on average by roughly 10 percent for more than 20 years after a displacement. The persistence of sizeable earnings losses is a challenge to most of the theories discussed above.

The ability of human capital theory to explain long-term earnings losses depends in part on the speed and the length of time over which specific human capital can be accumulated. Consider two workers who each had 10 years of tenure at an employer in year t, at which time worker A is laid off and worker B retains her position. Suppose further that worker A quickly finds a second job that he retains for the next ten years. Empirical research suggests that, on average, worker A should earn substantially less than worker B even after that second 10 year period. For specific human capital to explain that, it would have to be that it takes *more than 10* years to attain the maximum level of specific human capital within a firm. That seems to us to be a long time in most jobs – though there may be exceptions – but the fact is that we have little independent information with which to assess the validity of such an interpretation. Such a long period may be more plausible for the occupation- or industry-specific versions of those models. For instance, it seems plausible that a biostatistician working for a drug firm would still be learning new methods in biostatistics after 10 years in the business. But, again, relatively little is known about the types of skills that constitute industry- or occupation-specific human capital, let alone the speed with which those skills may be acquired, so there is a generous degree of speculation in any such judgment.

By the same token, for matching theories to explain such persistence in earnings losses, it must typically take 10 or more years to find a match that is near the top of the match-quality distribution. In the Jovanovic model, the speed with which workers find such matches is a function of both the variance in the distribution of job match qualities and in the speed with which employees and firms learn about the quality of matches. However, our view is that relatively little is known about those parameters, and furthermore they likely vary greatly across occupations.[19]

The persistence of measured earnings losses is also interesting from the perspective of models of backloaded compensation. Each of those models entails an early pay-in period followed by a payback period in which compensation exceeds productivity. Consider workers laid off from their jobs at the start of the payback period who immediately start new jobs that require them to go back to the start of the pay-in period. Such workers' displaced earnings will fall short of their non-displaced earnings for as long as the backloaded compensation "contract" calls for increasing earnings. If that contract's period of rising pay is very long, then earnings losses could continue for an equally long time. But if the terms of the implicit pay-in and payback periods are relatively short, as one might expect given the short median duration of new jobs in the United States, the long duration of lower earnings is a challenge for that backloaded compensation models. To our knowledge, however, there has been little effort to calibrate those periods, so there is relatively little basis on which to assess whether those models can explain long-term losses. It is worth noting, however, that Lazear's (1979) original model of backloaded compensation was designed to explain the existence of defined benefit pension plans and mandatory retirement rules that only come into play in long-term employment relationships. And, of course, both defined-benefit plans and mandatory retirement rules are now much less common than they were in the 1970s, suggesting that this mechanism may be less important than it once was.

Other theories considered here are more easily squared with long-term earnings losses. In some information-revelation models, displaced workers were, prior to their displacement, overpaid in relation to either their general or specific ability. The displacement revealed to them and to future employers that their productivity was not commensurate with their prior pay; as a result, their pay may never catch up that of observationally similar but more productive workers that were not laid off.

---

[19] Lange (2007) presents evidence that employers learn quickly about individual workers' productivity, but the focus there is on general skills rather than on skills or tastes that might be specific to a worker-firm match.

Theories based on rents can also generate persistent earnings losses for displaced workers. As noted above, a simple version of such models may have two employment sectors – a high-paid "rent" sector and a lower-paid "competitive" sector – and workers are periodically shuffled between the two sectors because of displacements and hires. Some workers displaced from the rent sector may ultimately regain their position, but displaced workers will on average be paid less in perpetuity as long as some of them are forced to work in the lower-pay competitive sector. Note that the costliness of displacement in such a model is contingent on the rate of displacement being higher in the rent sector. Displacements that simply shift an equal number of workers between the rent and the competitive sectors would not lead to an average cost of displacement in either the short or the long term.

Theories based on household reallocation also offer some promise of explaining long-run effects. Also, it has long been recognized that job displacement may alter the distribution of work within households – the added worker effect – though most of that research appears to have studied short-run responses of spouses and other family members to layoffs of others. One study of that effect found that increased earnings of wives offset 25 percent of the earnings losses of their displaced husbands (Stephens, 2002). Those effects might be quite persistent, however, as household roles may permanently mold to changes in spouses' earnings capacities.

Given that health has been demonstrated to affect earnings, there is a fairly direct transmission mechanism from the job displacement to long-term earnings losses from that perspective. There are two related mechanisms that explain how an adverse health effect of displacement can lead to long-term earnings losses. First, displacement may have a direct – that is, not mediated through earnings – long-run effect on health, and diminished health may lead to lower earnings in the long run. Second, displacement may directly have only a short-run effect on health, but that short-run effect can propagate longer-run adverse effects on earnings because of lost opportunities to develop work experience. Those longer-run earnings effects may, in turn, lower health levels in the long-run.

The Range of Earnings Changes is Wide

Many displaced workers have greatly reduced earnings, while some displaced workers earn *more* after their displacement (Carrington, 1993; Schoeni and Dardia 1996; Fallick, Haltiwanger, and McEntarfer 2012). Variance in outcomes may of course be explained by measurement error in survey data, but the range of outcomes is wide even when measured in relatively accurate administrative earnings data. The wide range of outcomes cannot be explained solely by a model in which human capital is only specific to a firm; within the confines of that model a displacement cannot lead to higher earnings. A wide range of outcomes is more consistent with models in which human capital is specific to industries or occupations. In that case, workers that lose their jobs at a particular firm but who quickly find similar work elsewhere are not displaced on any dimension that matters to them (Neal, 1995), so the stability of earnings in response to some displacements is not surprising. However, even here there is no natural explanation for why some workers' earnings would *increase* after a displacement; the best that could be hoped for would be a lateral move that left earnings unchanged.

The wide range of outcomes is more favorable to theories of matching. If the distribution of potential job-worker matches is wide, then so will be the distribution of displacement-induced earnings changes, including gains as well as losses.[20] That occurs in a matching model because workers don't simply search for the absolute best match available; instead, workers apply a stopping rule, whereby they suspend the search upon finding jobs that exceed their reservation quality. Thus, some displaced workers are lucky and find an exceptional match quickly after displacement.

Theories of backloaded compensation can explain a range of outcomes if workers are displaced at varying tenures relative to their "payback" points, and some move to jobs with a degree of back-loading that differs from that of the job from which they were displaced. To take a very simple example, suppose that there are two types of jobs available – backloaded-pay jobs where pay steps up linearly from $10 to $20 per hour over a course of ten years, and standard-pay jobs that pay $15 per hour at all times. Workers laid off in the ninth year of a backloaded-pay job would see their hourly wages fall from $19 per hour to either $15 or $10 per hour depending upon the type of new job taken. A worker laid off in the third year of a backloaded-pay job, however, would see his hourly wage either rise to $15 or fall to $10 depending upon the type of new job he took. In contrast, theories of information-revelation – the idea that being

---

[20] There is reason to believe that the distribution is, indeed, quite wide. See Low, Meghir, and Pistaferri (2010).

displaced signals low worker quality to potential future employers – are hard to square with an increase in earnings and wages.

Theories of rent could explain variability if the level of rents varies from job to job but, again, to explain earnings gains would require that workers be displaced from a low-rent job and then to find reemployment at a high-rent job. That is clearly possible, but it would not seem to be a common event, whereas earnings gains following displacement are fairly common.

Theories of household reallocation and health are consistent with a wide range of losses if households reorganize themselves in heterogeneous ways after a displacement or if the effects of displacement on workers' health are heterogeneous; both are reasonable propositions. Such theories, however, also have trouble explaining how earnings could rise with displacement. We are aware, for example, of no simple model of household reallocation that would predict that displacement by a spouse would lead to substitution towards more work by that same spouse. Similarly, we are aware of no theory of how job displacement improves health and, by extension, earnings capacity. While more of a measurement issue than a theory, another partial explanation for observed earnings gains is that some displaced workers take new jobs whose non-wage amenities are worse but whose earnings are higher. The available evidence does not support that as an explanation for average losses, but it may help explain why earnings rise for a subset of workers. A hypothetical example would be a worker displaced from a low-wage job in Hawaii (high non-wage amenities) who then moves to high-wage Alaska (low non-wage amenities). Such a worker could be worse off even if their earnings rose.

Virtually any theory of costly displacement can accommodate a range of outcomes if the theory is assumed to apply to some displaced workers but not to others. Meaningful use of any such "partial" theory, however, requires the development of an understanding of when the theory applies and when it doesn't. There is some tradition within the empirical literature that recognizes that possibility, as some analysts have, for example, chosen to exclude workers displaced from the construction industry from their analyses, on the grounds that there are relatively few persistent employment relationships in that industry (e.g., Kletzer, 1996). Some analysts (Carrington 1993) have examined variability in earnings losses across industries in the hope of pinning down the specific portions of the economy where particular theories might apply, but it seems accurate to say that the literature has not successfully paired off particular displaced workers with particular theories.

Earnings Losses Increase With the "Degree" of Displacement.

Displacement is often viewed as a dichotomous outcome: Workers are either displaced or not displaced based on the nature of her separation from the employer. But the literature has considered whether there are degrees of displacement, where the degree is determined by either pre-displacement job tenure or a measure of the similarity between the pre-and post-displacement jobs. Following are examples of relevant empirical work:

- Many studies have shown that earnings losses are highest for workers who had high tenure on their pre-displacement jobs, although the literature is not in complete agreement on that point (Kletzer, 1989; Topel, 1990; Carrington 1993; von Wachter, Song, and Manchester 2009). Also, pre-displacement job tenure is positively correlated with post-displacement earnings levels (for instance, Addison and Portugal 1989; Kletzer 1991).

- Many studies have shown that earnings losses are larger for workers who switch industry, occupation, or region than for measurably similar workers who find new work in the same general area as their former jobs (Addison and Portugal 1989; Ong and Mar 1992; Jacobson, LaLonde, and Sullivan, 1993; Carrington 1993; Neal, 1995; Couch and Placzek, 2010). Moreover, post-displacement earnings rise more with same-sector tenure than with other-sector tenure (Neal 1995; Kletzer, 1996), and post-displacement earnings of workers re-employed in the same industry rise with pre-displacement tenure to a similar degree as did pre-displacement earnings (Ong and Mar 1992; Neal, 1995).

- Industry-switching is less common from industries with more specialized occupations, suggesting that specialized workers are particularly reluctant to learn new work that may entail starting out at a low wage (Kletzer, 1992; Kletzer, 1996).

- The earnings loss/job tenure relationship is attenuated in circumstances where the local conditions – defined by industry, occupation, or locale – are themselves not bad. That is, there are other similar employers that continue to offer employment (Carrington, 1993).

- Displaced workers who are unexpectedly recalled to their pre-displacement employers saw substantial earnings reductions, although not as large as did those who were not recalled. (Kodrzycki 2007; Fujita and Moscarini 2013).

The results on tenure are most directly consistent with specific human capital and job matching theories, which were in part constructed to explain rising wage/seniority profiles. High-tenure workers have had time to accumulate (and then lose) the most human capital that was specific to their pre-displacement employer, and high-tenure workers may be those who are most well-matched to their jobs and for whom the loss of the job is therefore most costly. The result on unexpected recalls also seems most consistent with depreciation or obsolescence of human capital. Models in which human capital or match-quality is specific to an industry or occupation, rather than to a single firm, are more consistent with the other findings on gradations of displacement.

The increase in losses with tenure also has a direct interpretation within models of backloaded compensation. The tie between losses and industry- (or occupation-) switching and between losses and same-sector tenure, however, suggests that backloaded compensation models cannot be the whole story, because in those models it is of no consequence whether or not any subsequent employer is similar to the prior employer. Even an identically situated new employer will feel no obligation to repay an employee's implicit bond that has been paid into and then lost from a prior employer. In a similar fashion, the degree of displacement has little interpretation within theories of earnings loss based on information revelation. If a prior employer signals that laid off workers are of low quality, then that signal would seem to be roughly as informative to all potential new employers, not just those in dissimilar areas of activity. Indeed, a prior employer's signal that their former worker was low-quality might be most important to similar employers, whose production processes are most similar to those of the pre-displacement employer.

Employer rents may jointly explain both displacement-induced losses and their correlation with prior job tenure. In particular, high-rent jobs may both induce jobholders to stay in their positions for as long as possible and lead to large losses when and if those positions are lost. In contrast, it appears to us that theories of household reallocation have no implications for the relationship between earnings losses and the degree of displacement. The role of health in this

28

context not been heavily explored, though Sullivan and von Wachter (2009) find that the adverse effects of displacement on mortality are not sensitive to the variation of sample restrictions based on job tenure. Still, it seems possible that the loss of a long-term job is more depressing than the loss of one held for a shorter time-period, and that this might in turn explain some of the relationship between job tenure and displacement-induced earnings losses.

A switch in emphasis from displacement from job to displacement from industry or occupation may still be too simple a categorization of the circumstances facing displaced workers. In a manner similar to Lazear's (2009) generalization of specific human capital theory, some recent work has examined the "skill portfolio" – the mix of skills used – of both pre- and post-displacement jobs, and measured the "distance" between the two (Poletaev and Robinson, 2008). The results suggest that switching industry or occupation *per se* is less important than switching skill portfolio. Earnings losses tend to be larger when the post-displacement job requires a different skill portfolio than the old job. That perspective, too, would seem to favor human capital or matching theories, though again the specificity would likely be to something broader than a single firm.[21]

Earnings Losses Vary by Amount of Schooling and Training

Earnings of college graduates fall proportionally by less than do the earnings of the less educated or those with specialized degrees (von Wachter, Handwerker and Hildreth 2009; but also see Stevens 1997). Education does not play a central role in any of the theories discussed above, so the implications of that result for various theories are not obvious. There is a branch of human capital theory, however, which hypothesizes that an important benefit of education is that it enables educated workers to respond more easily to changes in technology in particular and to the economic environment in general (for instance, Welch 1970, Schultz 1975). Relatedly, there is some evidence that wage rates tend to rise more steeply with education in industries with more rapid technical change (Gill, 1989). The result that displacement is less costly for more highly educated workers thus fits well within a suitably broadened theory of human capital. Several

---

[21] In a related vein, if displacements attributable to technological change induced the greatest earnings losses, that would argue in favor of a human capital explanation. Aaronson and Housinger (1999) and Song (2009) suggest that the "position abolished" category in the Displaced Worker Survey is more likely to be associated with technological change, and more likely to be associated with higher levels of human capital. At this point, however, an interaction between technological change and lost human capital has not been established.

studies have found that earnings losses of displaced workers are higher in industries where on-the-job training is common (Jacobson, LaLonde and Sullivan, 1993; Carrington and Zaman, 1994; Schoeni and Dardia, 1996), which is most readily interpreted within the context of specific human capital models. However, those studies also found earnings losses to be higher in industries in which average wages are high, many workers are unionized, and firms are large, which are all most suggestive of rents or backloaded compensation models.

Earnings Losses Depend on Macroeconomic Conditions

The long-run effect of displacement on earnings depends upon both general and local economic conditions. Workers displaced during recessions typically have larger initial earnings losses than do workers displaced during better macroeconomic times (Topel 1990; Farber 1993; Couch and Placzek 2010; Couch, Jolly and Placzek 2011). The macroeconomic effect on outcomes is not fleeting either, as might be expected if displaced workers' earnings were simply depressed along with those of all other labor market participants. Instead, the effect is quite persistent even after macroeconomic conditions improve (Couch, Jolly, and Placzek, 2011; Davis and von Wachter, 2011). Displaced workers' earnings losses are also related to the local economic conditions in which the displacement took place. Numerous studies have shown that earnings losses are lower when the displacement occurs in better labor demand conditions defined at the "local" (as defined by industry and/or geography) level (Howland and Peterson 1988; Jacobson, LaLonde, and Sullivan, 1993; Carrington 1993; Kodrzycki 1995; Davis and von Wachter 2011).[22] So, losing a job in bad times and places is worse than losing a job in good times and places.

The long-lasting effects of macroeconomic conditions on earnings losses at the time of displacement do not differentiate strongly among the theories reviewed here, but may be most favorable to matching theories, as bad times may force a displaced worker to re-start the matching process from a lower rung on the job ladder. However, that finding may also be consistent with the Oyer and Schaefer (2000) model of information-revelation, in which employers retain their marginally overvalued employees until they can lay them off and credibly claim that the dismissals were due to weak demand. In that case, prospective subsequent

---

[22] Note, however, that Nakamura (2008) contends that average wage losses are lower when the unemployment rate is higher because the pool of displaced workers is of higher quality.

employers may be particularly suspicious about the quality of workers laid off in periods of weak demand, because those are the times when firms lay off their weak performers. The finding would seem to be most difficult to reconcile with theories of backloaded compensation, as we see no obvious reason why generally worse times should be associated with job losses concentrated in jobs with backloaded compensation schemes.

In a related vein, tighter labor market conditions have persistent positive effects on earnings at a continuously held job which are lost upon displacement. In particular, wage rates or weekly earnings at a job are higher when the minimum (state) unemployment rate during the worker's tenure at that job was lower (Beaudry and DiNardo 1991; Grant 2003). Relatedly, earnings losses following displacement are larger when the minimum unemployment rate during the pre-displacement job was lower (Schmieder and von Wachter 2010). In short, rates of pay within a worker's tenure on a job appear to ratchet up when labor markets are tight, but that gain is lost upon displacement. That finding may be consistent with theories of firm-specific human capital, matching, or rents: Tighter labor markets during a worker's tenure at a job may put that worker in a better bargaining position, leading to the quasi-rents from specific human capital investment or good matches, or, indeed, true rents, to be split more in favor of the worker.

It is also true that tighter labor markets would be consistent with a larger number of outside opportunities, in which case continued tenure at a job signals a better match in cross-section comparisons. However, the probability of displacement from a job also rises with the minimum unemployment rate during the time at that job (Schmieder and von Wachter 2010), which does not favor a pure matching explanation.[23] Thus, those combined findings would be more consistent with theories of rents or quasi-rents (from specific human capital or perhaps match quality) if combined with some kind of downward wage rigidity.

Part of Earnings Losses is Due to Reduced Employment

Displaced workers spend less time employed following displacement than does the general working population (Farber 1993). One study finds the differences are smaller in good times than bad, and fade away in four or so years following displacement (Ruhm, 1991). That result is consistent with any theory of earning losses, at least provided that reservation wages are slow to

---

[23]In addition, the probability of quitting falls (Grant 2003), which is consistent with any of those three theories.

adjust following job loss. That is, if displaced workers do not fully adjust their reservation wages to the lower earnings opportunities that follow from loss of human capital, match quality, tenure, reputation, or health, then more time spent unemployed would be expected.

A related cost of displacement is that displacement increases one's subsequent risk of displacement, which exacerbates long-term earnings losses (Stevens 1997). Theories of matching or of specific human capital (as a glue that prevents job loss) can explain both future displacements and why those future displacements prevent workers from recovering lost earnings. Future employers will likely use a last-in-first-out approach to any future layoff and the recently displaced will be among the last-in. Models of deferred compensation and rents do not readily explain an increase in future displacements. Theories of information-revelation could explain increased subsequent rates of job loss if subsequent employers do not fully incorporate into their expectations about an employee's productivity the information about that productivity implicit in their prior displacement. Subsequent employers may not incorporate that information, for example, if they are not aware of the employee's prior displacement, in which case the new employer may have to relearn what was already known to the prior employer.

There is disagreement in the literature about the importance of reduced employment relative to lower wage rates and shorter workweeks in accounting for earnings losses. Davis and von Wachter (2011) and Ruhm (1991) find that long-term losses in earnings are concentrated in lower wage rates and shorter workweeks, not in lack of full-time employment; Schoeni and Dardia (1996) find that losses are concentrated in reduced workweeks and employment, not in lower wage rates; Kessel and Maher (1991) found no effect on weekly hours in a case study in Vermont.[24] Even a clear answer to the margins along which losses occur in the aggregate would probably not be of much help in distinguishing among theories. However, temporary and part-time jobs after displacement tend to be steps in a transition path to new regular and full-time jobs (Farber 1999). That finding is most favorable to models of job matching, but is consistent with other theories as well.

---

[24] The roles of reduced employment and reduced wage rates vary substantially across developed countries. See Burda and Mertens (2001); Kuhn (2002); and Hijzen, Upward and Wright (2010).

Gibbons and Katz (1991) found that among white-collar workers but not blue-collar workers, those displaced by plant closings had smaller wage losses and shorter unemployment spells than those displaced from continuing firms, which they interpreted as favorable to theories of information-revelation. This result, however, has not been uniformly replicated in subsequent analyses. Hu and Taber (2011), for example, found that while this result holds for white men, it is reversed for women and black men, for whom other factors (such as discrimination) may play a larger role. Other studies have found patterns similar to Gibbons and Katz but have further explored the mechanics of their findings. Stevens (1997), for example, found that the smaller earnings losses for those displaced by plant closings arose because such workers' earnings fell prior to displacement. Krashinsky (2002) found that the smaller earnings losses for those displaced by plant closings is a result of plants that close tending to have been smaller and to have paid less to begin with. Finally, Song (2007) found that the appearance of the white collar/blue collar distinction in Gibbons and Katz's study resulted from recall bias in the 1984 and 1986 Displaced Worker Surveys, and that no plant-closing differential was present in the 2000 and 2002 Surveys in which recall bias was less severe.

The original evidence on difference in earnings losses following more severe firm distress was put forth in support of a theory of information revelation. Subsequent empirical research has not consistently replicated that original result, however. The lack of consistency is perhaps not surprising given the quite contrary predictions provided by other theories. In particular, the order in which workers "flee the sinking ship" is related to the relative quality of their outside opportunities. Workers that are highly specialized to their pre-displacement employer, either through specific human capital or job matching, or workers in the midst of being paid back their implicit bond will be slow to leave struggling employers, whereas those with little attachment to their employer will leave at the first sign of employer distress. These theories then, in contrast to the information revelation theory, suggest that the workers that stick around until the final plant closure will be those with the most to lose. There is thus a theoretical tension between theories that emphasize firms pushing low-performers out the door as soon as possible and theories that emphasize highly-specialized workers clinging to their employer for as long as possible. The mixed empirical evidence suggests to us that each of these views has some validity and that, by extension, no single theory can explain patterns for all workers and all firms.

Earnings Losses Differ by Demographics

Employment falls after displacement for workers over 55, often permanently, suggesting that displacement hastens retirement. This is especially true among married women, while the opposite may be true among older men (Chan and Stevens 1999; Chan and Stevens 2001; Rodriguez and Zavodny 2001; Chan and Stevens 2004). Unmarried women have post-displacement outcomes similar to those of men, whereas married women, especially those with young children, have less employment and shorter hours post-displacement. Otherwise, there are few sex differences in wage losses (Rodriguez and Zavodny 2001). Those demographic differences in accelerated retirement and other reductions in employment and hours suggest that intra-household reallocation is at work, but the impetus for that reallocation may stem from reductions in earnings opportunities attributable to any of the other theories of earnings loss.

The earnings losses of young displaced workers are similar to those of older workers, but their relative losses become smaller as time goes by. Unlike for older workers, lower subsequent earnings growth (relative to the control group) is a major component of long-run losses for young adults (Kletzer and Fairlie 2003). Age-related differences in displacement-related changes in earnings invite the consideration of displacement within the overall context of workers' careers. At the two extremes, workers displaced in the first or last week of their careers see virtually no change in their career earnings, with the youthful worker able to quickly embark on employment with a new employer if aggregate conditions allow and the older worker losing at most a week's pay. In between those two extremes, the costs of displacement surely rise considerably with age before ultimately falling as retirement nears, taking on a shape similar to the familiar Laffer Curve. Like that other curve, however, the precise shape of the empirical relationship between age and the lifetime costs of displacement are not well-understood.

Displacement Harms Health

There is now ample evidence that displacement adversely affects health. Sullivan and von Wachter (2009) found significant differences in death rates and life expectancy between displaced workers and a control group. For high-tenure male workers, they found that mortality rates were increased by 50% to 100% in the year after displacement. Mortality rates were less elevated in years further removed from the displacement, but their results suggest that displacement reduces a worker's life expectancy by 1 to 1½ years for mid-career males. Further, the increases in mortality rates are highest for workers whose earnings decreased the most. Those results admit to two non-exclusive interpretations. First, the lower earnings induced by displacement – via some non-health-related mechanism possibly – increases mortality because mortality is negatively correlated with income (for example, Deaton and Paxson, 2001). That is, displacement makes you poorer and being poorer reduces life expectancy. Second, displacement may harm health and those events may in turn reduce income. In short, displacement makes you sick, and that reduces your earnings. Of course, both mechanisms may be at work and mutually reinforcing.

The mechanics of how job displacement affects mortality are not well understood, but the empirical literature suggests a strong role for mental health. Though not directly tied to job displacement per se, Davis and von Wachter (2011) documented a large increase in anxiety among workers during the recent recession, and, in an earlier study, Kessler, House and Turner (1987) found heightened incidence of mental health issues in recently laid-off workers. Krueger and Mueller (2012), in a survey of workers from New Jersey, found that unemployed workers report high levels of sadness and that their mood improves significantly upon reemployment. In a study of Norwegian workers, Black, Deveraux and Salvanes (2012) found that displacement is associated with an elevated incidence of coronary disease, in part precipitated by an increase in smoking. In a study of Swedish workers, Eliason and Storrie (2009) found that workers displaced in plant closures are at increased risk of alcoholism and, particularly among men, are at increased risk of traffic accidents and self-harm. Charles and Stephens (2004) found that job displacement leads to a heightened risk of divorce, whereas, in contrast, the onset of disability does not, even though both lead to reduced earnings. Those results are consistent with the view that job displacement has consequences for mental health that are not themselves the result of reduced earnings.

The effects of job displacement on mental health may be one reason that displacement adversely affects the children of displaced workers (Oreopoulos, Page, and Stevens 2008). Children's earnings, of course, are generally increasing in their parents' income, so part of the effect of job displacement on the adult outcomes of the displaced worker's children may be due to the fact that displacement reduces their parents' income (see, for example, Lee and Solon 2009). But it is reasonable to suppose that part of the effect of parental job displacement on children's later earnings may be due a reduction in effective parental inputs into, loosely speaking, the child's human capital. That latter view is supported by the work of Rege, Telle and Votruba (2011), who found that the displacement of Norwegian fathers (though not mothers) had an adverse effect on their children's school performance independent of its effect on family income.

There is clearly, then, a strong nexus between health (particularly mental health), earnings, and job displacement. Although the causality between health and earnings outcomes probably runs in both directions, our reading of the literature indicates that at least a substantial part runs from reduced health to reduced earnings. Most policy interventions studied by economists have tended to focus, not surprisingly, on conventionally "economic" policies such as job search assistance, job training, and unemployment and earnings insurance. But if a primary driving factor behind the difficulties of displaced workers is mental health, then policies that mitigate the mental effects of job displacement may be more effective. One study, for example, found that job-search assistance paired with psychological interventions such as problem-solving training and social reinforcement worked better than job-search assistance alone (Caplan, Vinokur, Price and van Ryn, 1989). Mental health does not play a role in any of the more conventional models of earnings levels and changes, with the partial exception of the very general model of Benabou and Tirole (2002).

IV. Implications

Table 2 summarizes the empirical findings and their implications for the theories. As we have emphasized, a range of theories have something to say about why earnings fall for displaced workers, but little of the evidence is strongly differentiating and no theory provides a full explanation on its own. Models of specific human capital, for example, do well at explaining the tenure profile of earnings losses, but they are hard to square with earnings gains upon displacement. Moreover, they rely on the assumption that there is a significant component of earnings power that is truly firm- or industry-specific, an assumption that in some cases seems hard to support. Models of matching can explain the tenure profile of losses and can also explain earnings that increase with displacement, but, like specific human capital models, they have trouble explaining the extremely long duration of earnings losses. Models of backloaded compensation also explain the tenure profile of earnings losses, but they are intrinsically models of firm-specific earnings capacity and do not easily explain the role of industry-switching or local market conditions in the losses of displaced workers. Models of worker rents can explain the persistence of reduced earnings among displaced workers, but cannot easily explain wage gains upon displacement, the variation of earnings losses with "degrees" of displacement, or, obviously, the presence of losses among workers who were likely not receiving pre-displacement rents. Models of information-revelation can explain the persistence of earnings losses but do not directly explain the tenure profile of losses. Intrahousehold reallocation can explain substantial long-term losses for displaced workers whose household arrangements change with displacement, but research finds substantial earnings losses for people for whom such arrangements are unlikely to be important, so that too is an incomplete explanation. Finally, the decline in health – both physical and mental – that often accompanies a displacement can potentially explain a wide range of post-displacement outcomes, but it, too, cannot easily explain wage gains, and is unsatisfactory as a standalone explanation in part because we then need a theory of why displacement harms health.

The relative weights that one puts on the various models matter from several perspectives. First, while it is clear that most displaced workers' earnings fall relative to what they would have earned in the absence of the displacement, it is less clear that, relative to the expectations with which they began the job from which they were displaced, workers came out worse than they expected upon accession to those jobs. No job is expected to last forever when it begins, and so workers presumably make some forecast about how long jobs will last. In the models of specific human capital, matching or, especially, backloaded compensation, those who remain on the job the longest lose the most instantaneously upon displacement but were, at the same time, more fortunate than those who might have been displaced at earlier stages of their career at the employer. Thus, whether displaced workers were unfortunate in the totality of their experience on the job depends greatly on the point in their anticipated job tenure path at which they were displaced.

Theories of information revelation offer a different perspective on whether displaced workers with the largest earnings losses were the most unlucky. In those models, displaced workers with the largest losses are those who were most overpaid at their prior job. Workers may be overpaid prior to displacement because the employer made a mistake in its initial salary offer, or because worker performance deteriorated over time. If workers' overpaid status is a function of mistakes made in the hiring process, then workers displaced because they were overpaid may have had the most luck in finding the job from which they were ultimately displaced. That is true even though their earnings fall with displacement, and a few years of overly high pay is better than no such years.

The extent to which displacement entails a social loss varies from theory to theory. Human capital explanations generally suggest that most displacements are efficient in that work effort is reallocated towards more productive uses. Some analysts (such as Lalonde, 2007) view wage insurance as a price that should be paid to individuals bearing losses so as to make reallocations towards more productive uses more palatable, in addition to its more direct insurance value. But if displacements have long-term health effects that are not considered or fully appreciated by either firms (in their decisions on when to displaced workers) or workers (in their decisions on whether to accept lower wages in lieu of displacement), then displacements may be inefficient. Displacements may also, at the margin, be inefficient in models of long-term contracting, in that firms that lay workers off may confer a negative externality on other employers by making workers less likely to accept such arrangements.

Understanding why earnings fall with displacement can be helpful in formulating policy responses. Much of the policy discussion focuses on the role of short-run policy interventions such as unemployment insurance. But there is clearly a longer-run issue. Two of the most often discussed – and occasionally attempted – approaches to remediate long-run earnings losses for displaced workers are job training and longer-term wage insurance. Both of those policies seem to be motivated by the specific human capital view. But other perspectives on earnings losses potentially suggest alternative long-run responses. Earnings losses driven by information revelation, such as an implicit statement by the prior employer that the displaced worker was overpaid, do not immediately suggest a policy response on either equity or efficiency grounds. To the extent that earnings losses are driven by family reallocation, the magnitude of the policy response would probably be smaller than if earnings losses were caused for some other reasons, since many of the negative effect of displacement are offset within the family itself. And earnings losses driven by health, particularly mental health, suggest a different type of policy response altogether. One view is that workers in most firms work their way up "job ladders" that reflect some combination of specific human capital acquisition, matching and backloaded compensation, and that getting knocked off a ladder that has been partly climbed is costly to workers (von Wachter, 2010). We largely agree with that view, but we also believe that more widespread reflection about the range of potential interpretations would be useful. That reflection should include the other models discussed here, namely information revelation, household reallocation, and health impacts. As a profession we have many pieces of the puzzle for the mechanics by which earnings fall as a result of displacement, but we have not yet fit them together into a convincing narrative.

Some refocusing of future empirical research on evidence that would help differentiate among theories would also be useful. One obviously fruitful direction would be to replicate with other data some of the results discussed above in cases for which the evidence is currently thin, perhaps taking advantage of recent and ongoing advances in matched employer-employee and longitudinal administrative data, among other sources. Another approach would be to study the full path of earnings, over previous and subsequent jobs, with an eye toward a more rigorous evaluation of matching theories. Under matching, as opposed to human capital or agency theories, we would expect to see wage increases both before and after displacement concentrated during changes of employer or occupation.

A second, quite ambitious, agenda would identify and value sets of skills possessed by workers before displacement, and examine whether earnings losses upon displacement are associated with a change in the general market value of those skills. That would help to evaluate those theories that associate both displacement and the subsequent loss of earnings with declines in the value of particular skills in either aggregate or local labor markets, and distinguish them from matching theories in which the human capital itself has not depreciated in value, but earnings losses stem solely from the difficulty in finding a post-displacement match that conforms to a worker's set of skills.

Third, we think that further research into the experience of displaced workers who are unexpectedly recalled to their pre-displacement position holds promise. As noted above, such workers appear to experience substantial earnings reductions. However, interpretation of that result as favoring human capital theories over others depends upon whether those workers were recalled to their previous jobs in the traditional sense, or were treated as new hires – that is, brought back into a new (possibly two-tiered) wage structure, as some anecdotal evidence would have it. Perhaps such new structures could be identified for sufficiently large employers by discrete changes in the patterns of earnings of new hires.

In the end, however, we think that further empirical research is unlikely to ever fully tell us the weight that should be put on the various theories of displacement and earnings loss discussed above, or whether some quite different mechanism is at work. In their early 1980s review of the closely related question of why earnings typically grow over a person's career, Mincer and Jovanovic (1981) concluded that "a rough estimate is that fifty percent of lifetime wage growth is due to general (transferable) experience and twenty-five percent to firm-specific experience and interfirm mobility." We applaud the use of the "rough" modifier, but an additional thirty years of experience has not left us any closer to an authoritative and simple answer to the question of why earnings fall with job displacement, and, indeed, we suspect that Mincer and Jovanovic's rough apportionment was more uncertain than even a "rough" modifier would indicate. A more circumspect conclusion was offered by Hutchens (1989), who concluded his review article by noting that "we are a long way from a full understanding of seniority, wages, and productivity." It would be nice, twenty-five years later, to say that we have closed the gap between our knowledge and a full understanding. Yet while new statistical regularities have been developed and others extended, and while some new models have been advanced, the fact remains that, in our view, the economic interpretation of displaced workers' earnings losses remains uncertain.

References

Aaronson, Daniel, and Housinger, Kenneth. 1999. "The Impact of Technology on Displacement and Reemployment," *Economic Perspectives – Federal Reserve Bank of Chicago*, vol. 23, pp. 14-30.

Acemoglu, Daron, and Robert Shimer. 2000. "Productivity gains from unemployment insurance," *European Economic Review* 44(7), pp. 1195-1224.

Addison, John T., and Blackburn, McKinley L. 2000. "The Effects of Unemployment Insurance on Post-unemployment Earnings," *Labour Economics* 7(1), pp. 21-53.

Addison, John T., and Portugal, Pedro. 1989. "Job Displacement, Relative Wage Changes, and Duration of Unemployment," *Journal of Labor Economics* 7(3), pp. 281-302.

Addison, John T., and Portugal, Pedro. 1992. "Advance Notice and Unemployment: New Evidence from the 1988 Displaced Worker Survey," *Industrial and Labor Relations Review* 45(4), pp. 645-664.

Altonji, Joseph G., and Robert A. Shakotko. 1987. "Do Wages Rise with Job Seniority?" *Review of Economic Studies* 54(3), pp. 437-459.

Autor, David H., Donohue III, John J., and Schwab, Stewart J. 2006. "The Costs of Wrongful-Discharge Laws," *Review of Economics and Statistics*, 88(2), pp. 211-231.

Becker, Gary. 1962. Human Capital. University of Chicago Press.

Benabou, Roland, and Tirole, Jean. 2002. "Self-Confidence and Personal Motivation," *Quarterly Journal of Economics*117(3), pp. 871-915.

Bewley, Truman. 1999, Why Wages Don't Fall During a Recession. Harvard University Press.

Black, Sandra E., Deveraux, Paul J., and Salvanes, Kjell G. 2012. "Losing Heart? The Effect of Job Displacement on Health," IZA working paper, December.

Blanchflower, David, Oswald, Andrew J. and Sanfey, Peter. 1996. "Wages, Profits and Rent-Sharing," *Quarterly Journal of Economics* 111(1), pp. 227-251.

Bowlus, Audra and Lars Vilhuber, 2002. "Displaced Workers, Early Leavers, and Re-employment Wages," Longitudinal Employer-Household Dynamics Technical paper No. TP-2002-18, November.

Burda, Michael C., and Antje Mertens. 2001. "Estimating Wage Losses of Displaced Workers in Germany," *Labour Economics* 8(1): pp. 15–41.

Bureau of Labor Statistics. 2014. Median weekly earnings of long-tenured displaced full-time wage and salary workers on their lost jobs and on jobs held at the time of the survey, 1984-2012, communication, June 6, 2014.

Burgess, Paul L., and Low, Stuart A. 1992. "Preunemployment Job Search and Advance Job Loss Notice," *Journal of Labor Economics*, vol. 10, no. 3, pp. 258-287.

Caplan, Robert D., Vinokur, Amiram D., Price, Richard H., and van Ryn, Michelle. 1989. "Job Seeking, Reemployment and Mental Health: A Randomized Field Experiment in Coping With Job Loss," *Journal of Applied Psychology* 74(5), pp. 759-769.

Carrington, William J. 1993. "Wage Losses for Displaced Workers: Is It Really the Firm That Matters?" *Journal of Human Resources* 28(3), pp. 435-462.

Carrington, William, and Zaman, Asad. 1994. "Interindustry Variation in the Costs of Job Displacement," *Journal of Labor Economics* 12(2), pp. 243-275.

Chan, Sewin, and Stevens, Ann Huff. 1999. "Employment and Retirement Following a Late-Career Job Loss," *American Economic Review* 89(2), pp. 211-216.

Chan, Sewin, and Stevens, Ann Huff. 2001. "Job Loss and Employment Patterns for Older Workers," *Journal of Labor Economics* 19(2), pp. 484-521.

Chan, Sewin, and Stevens, Ann Huff. 2004. "How Does Job Loss Affect the Timing of Retirement?" *Contributions to Economic Analysis and Policy* 3(1), pp. 1-24.

Charles, Kerwin Kofi, and Melvin Stephens Jr. 2004. "Job Displacement, Disability, and Divorce," *Journal of Labor Economics* 22(2), pp. 489-522.

Cooper, Daniel. 2013. "The Effect of Unemployment Duration on Future Earnings and Other Outcomes," Federal Reserve Bank of Boston Working Paper No. 13-8, October.

Couch, Kenneth A., and Placzek, Dana A. 2010. "Earnings Losses of Displaced Workers Revisited," *American Economic Review* 100(1), pp. 572-589.

Couch, Kenneth A., Jolly, Nicholas A., and Placzek, Dana W. 2011. "Earnings Losses of Displaced Workers and the Business Cycle: An Analysis with Administrative Data," *Economics Letters* 111(1), pp. 16-19.

Davis, Steven J. 1987. "Fluctuations in the Pace of Labor Reallocation," Carnegie-Rochester Conference Series on Public Policy. Vol. 27. North-Holland.

Davis, Steven J., and von Wachter, Till M. 2011. "Recessions and the Cost of Job Loss," *Brookings Papers on Economic Activity*, Fall, pp.1-55.

Deaton, Angus, and Christina Paxson, 2011. "Mortality, Education, Income, and Inequality among American Cohorts," in Themes in the Economics of Aging, NBER Conference Report series. Chicago and London: University of Chicago Press, pp. 129-165.

Dickens, William T., Katz, Lawrence, Lang, Kevin, and Summers, Lawrence H. 1989. "Employee Crime and the Monitoring Puzzle." *Journal of Labor Economics* 7(3), pp.331-347.

Eliason, Marcus, and Donald Storrie. 2009. "Job Loss Is Bad For Your Health–Swedish Evidence on Cause-specific Hospitalization Following Involuntary Job Loss." *Social Science & Medicine* 68(8), pp. 1396-1406.

Fallick, Bruce C. 1993. "The Industrial Mobility of Displaced Workers," *Journal of Labor Economics* 11(2), pp. 302-323.

Fallick, Bruce C. 1994. "The Endogeneity of Advance Notice and Fear of Destructive Attrition," *Review of Economics and Statistics* 76(2), pp. 378-384.

Fallick, Bruce, Haltiwanger, John, and McEntarfer, Erika. 2012. "Job-to-Job Flows and the Consequences of Job Separations," Federal Reserve Board Finance and Economics Discussion Series #2012-73, September.

Farber, Henry S. 1993. "The Incidence and Costs of Job Loss: 1982-91," *Brookings Papers on Economic Activity: Microeconomics* 1993(1), pp. 73-132.

Farber, Henry S. 1999. "Alternative and Part-Time Employment Arrangements as a Response to Job Loss." *Journal of Labor Economics* 17(4), pp. S142-169.

Flaaen, Aaron, Matthew D. Shapiro and Isaac Sorkin. 2013. "Reconsidering the Consequences of Worker Displacements: Survey versus Administrative Measurements," Working paper, University of Michigan, September 5.

Fujita, Shigeru and Giuseppe Moscarini. 2013. "Recalls and Unemployment," Federal Reserve Bank of Philadelphia Working Paper #14-3, November.

Gibbons, Robert, and Lawrence Katz. 1991. "Layoffs and Lemons," *Journal of Labor Economics*, 9(4), pp. 351-380.

Gill, Indermit. 1989. *Technological Change, Education and Obsolesence of Human Capital: Some Evidence for the US*. Dissertation, University of Chicago, Department of Economics.

Grant, Darren. 2003. "The Effect of Implicit Contracts on the Movement of Wages over the Business Cycle: Evidence from the National Longitudinal Surveys," *Industrial and Labor Relations Review* 56(3), pp. 393-408.

Hall, Robert E., and Edward P. Lazear. 1984. "The Excess Sensitivity of Layoffs and Quits to Demand." *Journal of Labor Economics* 2(2), pp. 233-257.

Hijzen, Alexander, Richard Upward, and Peter W. Wright. 2010. "The Income Losses of Displaced Workers," *Journal of Human Resources*, 45(1), pp. 243-69.

Hildreth, Andrew K.G., and Oswald, Andrew J. 1997. "Rent-Sharing and Wages: Evidence from Company and Establishment Panels," *Journal of Labor Economics* 15(2), pp. 318-337.

Howland, Marie, and Peterson, George E. 1988. "Labor Market Conditions and the Reemployment of Displaced Workers," *Industrial and Labor Relations Review* 42(1), pp. 109-122.

Hu, Luojia, and Taber, Christopher. 2011. "Displacement, Asymmetric Information, and Heterogeneous Human Capital," *Journal of Labor Economics* 29(1), pp. 113-152.

Hutchens, Robert M. 1989. "Seniority, Wages and Productivity: A Turbulent Decade," *Journal of Economic Perspectives* 3(4), pp. 49-64.

Jacobson, Louis S., LaLonde, Robert J., and Sullivan, Daniel G. 1993. "Earnings Losses of Displaced Workers," *American Economic Review* 83(4), pp. 685-709.

Jones, Stephen R.G., and Kuhn, Peter. 1995. "Mandatory Notice and Unemployment," *Journal of Labor Economics* 13(4), pp. 599-622.

Jovanovic, Boyan. 1979a. "Job Matching and the Theory of Turnover," *Journal of Political Economy* 87(5), pp. 972-990.

Jovanovic, Boyan. 1979b. "Firm-Specific Capital and Turnover," *Journal of Political Economy* 87(6), pp. 1246-1260.

Kahn, Lisa B. 2013. "Asymmetric Information Between Employers," *American Economic Journal: Applied Economics* 5(4), pp. 165–205.

Kessler, Ronald C., James S. House, and J. Blake Turner. 1987. "Unemployment and Health in a Community Sample," *Journal of Health and Social Behavior* 28(1), pp. 51-59.

Klein, Benjamin, Robert G. Crawford, and Armen A. Alchian. 1978. "Vertical Integration, Appropriable Rents, and the Competitive Contracting Process," *Journal of Law & Economics* 21(2), pp. 297-326.

Kletzer, Lori G. 1989. "Returns to Seniority after Permanent Job Loss," *American Economic Review* 79(3), pp. 536-543.

Kletzer, Lori G. 1992. "Industry Wage Differentials and Wait Unemployment," *Industrial Relations*, 31(2), pp. 250-269.

Kletzer, Lori G. 1996. "The Role of Sector-Specific Skills in Post-displacement Earnings," *Industrial Relations*, vol. 35, no. 4, pp. 473-490.

Kletzer, Lori G., and Rosen, Howard F. 2006. "Reforming Unemployment Insurance for the Twenty-First Century Workforce," Hamilton Project Discussion Paper 2006-06.

Kodrzycki, Yolanda K. 1995. "The Costs of Defense-related Layoffs in New England," *New England Economic Review*, March: pp. 3-23.

Kodrzycki, Yolanda K. 2007. "Using Unexpected Recalls to Examine the Long-Term Earnings Effects of Job Displacement," Working paper, Federal Reserve Bank of Boston.

Krashinsky, Harry. 2002. "Evidence on Adverse Selection and Establishment Size in the Labor Market," *Industrial and Labor Relations Review*, 56(1), pp. 84-96.

Krolikowski, Pawel. 2014. "Job Ladders and Earnings of Displaced Workers," manuscript, University of Michigan, March 2014.

Krueger, Alan B. 1991. "The Evolution of Unjust Dismissal Legislation in the United States," *Industrial and Labor Relations Review*, 44(4), pp. 644–660.

Krueger, Alan B., and Mueller, Andreas. 2012. "The Lot of the Unemployed: A Time Use Perspective," *Journal of the European Economic Association* 10(4), pp. 765-794.

Kuhn, Peter Joseph (ed). 2002. *Losing Work, Moving on: International Perspectives on Worker Displacement*, W.E. Upjohn Institute.

Laibson, David. 1997. "Golden Eggs and Hyperbolic Discounting," *Quarterly Journal of Economics*, 112(2), pp. 443-478.

Lalonde, Robert J. 2007. "The Case for Wage Insurance," Council on Foreign Relations.

Lange, Fabian. 2007. "The Speed of Employer Learning." *Journal of Labor Economics* 25(1), pp. 1-35.

Lazear, Edward. 1979. "Why Is There Mandatory Retirement?" *Journal of Political Economy*, 87(6), pp. 1261-1284.

Lazear, Edward. 1981. "Agency, Earnings Profiles, Productivity, and Hours Restrictions," *American Economic Review*, 71(4), pp. 606-620.

Lazear, Edward. 2009. "Firm-Specific Human Capital: A Skill-Weights Approach," *Journal of Political Economy*, 117(5), pp. 914-940.

Lee, Chul-In, and Solon, Gary. 2009. "Trends in Intergenerational Income Mobility," *The Review of Economics and Statistics*, 91(4), pp. 766-772.

Loewenstein, George, and Sicherman, Nachum. 1991. "Do Workers Prefer Increasing Wage Profiles?" *Journal of Labor Economics*, 9(1), pp. 67-84.

Loewenstein, George F., and Prelec, Drazen. 1993. "Preferences for Sequences of Outcomes." *Psychological Review*, 100(1), pp. 91-108.

Low, Hamish, Meghir, Costas and Pistaferri, Luigi. 2010. "Wage Risk and Employment Risk over the Life Cycle," *American Economic Review* 100(4), pp. 1432–1467

Lundberg, Shelley. 1985. "The Added Worker Effect," *Journal of Labor Economics*, 3(1), pp. 11-37.

McLaughlin, Kenneth J. 1991. "A Theory of Quits and Layoffs with Efficient Turnover," *Journal of Political Economy*, 99(1), pp. 1-29.

Michaud, Amanda M. 2014. "An Information Theory of Worker Flows and Wage Dispersion," Manuscript, Indiana University, March 2014.

Mincer, Jacob. 1962. "On-the-Job Training: Costs, Returns, and Some Implications," *Journal of Political Economy*, 70(5), pp. 50-79.

Mincer, Jacob and Jovanovic, Boyan. 1981. "Labor Mobility and Wages." In *Studies in Labor Markets*, (Sherwin Rosen, Ed.), University of Chicago Press.

Murphy, Kevin M. 1986. "Specialization and Human Capital." Ph.D. Thesis University of Chicago.

Murphy, Kevin M., and Topel, Robert. 1990. "Efficiency Wages Reconsidered: Theory and Evidence," *Advances in the Theory and Measurement of Unemployment*, pp. 204-240.

Nakamura, Emi. 2008. "Layoffs and Lemons Over the Business Cycle," *Economics Letters*, 99(1), pp. 55-58.

Neal, Derek. 1995. "Industry-Specific Human Capital: Evidence from Displaced Workers," *Journal of Labor Economics*, 13(4), pp. 653-677.

Neal, Derek. 1999. "The Complexity of Job Mobility Among Young Men," *Journal of Labor Economics*, 17(2), pp. 237-261.

Nord, Stephen, and Ting, Yuan. 1991. "Impact of Advance Notice of Plant Closings on Earnings and Probability of Unemployment," *Industrial and Labor Relations Review*, 44(4), pp. 681-91.

Oi, Walter. 1962. "Labor as a Quasi-Fixed Factor," *Journal of Political Economy*, 70(6), pp. 538-555.

Ong, Paul M., and Mar, Don. 1992. "Post-Layoff Earnings Among Semiconductor Workers," *Industrial and Labor Relations Review*, 45(2), pp. 366-379.

Oreopoulos, Philip, Page, Marianne, and Stevens, Ann Huff. 2008. "The Intergenerational Effects of Worker Displacement," *Journal of Labor Economics*, 26(3), pp. 455-500.

Oyer, Paul, and Schaefer, Scott. 2000. "Layoffs and Litigation," *Rand Journal of Economics,* 31(2) pp. 345–358.

Poletaev, Maxim, and Robinson, Chris. 2008. "Human Capital Specificity: Evidence from the Dictionary of Occupational Titles and Displaced Worker Surveys, 1984-2000," *Journal of Labor Economics*, 26(3), pp. 387-420.

Rege, Mari, Telle, Kjetil, and Votruba, Mark. 2011. "Parental Job Loss and Children's School Performance," *Review of Economic Studies*, 78(4), pp. 1462-1489.

Rodriguez, Daniel, and Zavodny, Madeline. 2001. "Family Structure and Sex Differences in Postdisplacement Outcomes." Federal Reserve Bank of Atlanta Working Paper No. 2001-14.

Ruhm, Christopher. 1991. "Are Workers Permanently Scarred by Job Displacements?" *American Economic Review*, 81(1), pp. 319-324.

Ruhm, Christopher. 1992. "Advance Notice, Job Search, and Postdisplacement Earnings," *Journal of Labor Economics*, 10(1), pp. 1-32.

Ruhm, Christopher. 1994. "Advance Notice and Postdisplacement Joblessness," *Journal of Labor Economics*, 12(1), pp. 1-28.

Salop, Joanne, and Salop, Steven. 1976. "Self-Selection and Turnover in the Labor Market," *Quarterly Journal of Economics*, 90(4), pp. 619-627.

Schmieder, Johannes, and Von Wachter, Till. "Does Wage Persistence Matter for Employment Fluctuations? Evidence from Displaced Workers," *American Economic Journal: Applied Economics* 2(3), pp. 1-21.

Schoeni, Robert, and Dardia, Michael. 1996. "Earnings Losses of Displaced Workers in the 1990s," Working paper, RAND.

Schultz, Theodore W. 1975. "The Value of the Ability to Deal with Disequilibria," *Journal of Economic Literature*, 13(3), pp. 827-846.

Schwerdt, Guido. 2011. "Labor Turnover Before Plant Closure: 'Leaving the Sinking Ship' vs. 'Captain Throwing Ballast Overboard'," *Labour Economics* 18(1), pp. 93-101.

Shapiro, Carl, and Stiglitz, Joseph. 1984. "Equilibrium Unemployment as a Worker Discipline Device," *American Economic Review*, 74(3), pp. 433-444.

Shaw, Kathryn L. 1984. "A Formulation of the Earnings Function Using the Concept of Occupational Investment," *Journal of Human Resources*, 19(3), pp. 319-340.

Song, Younghwan. 2007. "Recall Bias in the Displaced Worker Survey: Are Layoffs Really Lemons?" *Labour Economics*, 14(3), pp. 334-345.

Song, Younghwan. 2009. "Training, Technological Changes and Displacement," *Journal of Labor Research*, 30(3), pp. 201-218.

Spence, Michael. 1973. "Job Market Signaling," *Quarterly Journal of Economics*, 87(3), pp. 355-374.

Stephens, Jr., Melvin. 2002. "Worker Displacement and the Added Worker Effect," *Journal of Labor Economics*, 20(3), pp. 504-537.

Stevens, Ann Huff. 1997. "Persistent Effects of Job Displacement: The Importance of Multiple Job Losses," *Journal of Labor Economics*, 15(1), pp. 165-188.

Sullivan, Daniel, and von Wachter, Till. 2009. "Job Displacement and Mortality: An Analysis Using Administrative Data," *Quarterly Journal of Economics*, 124(3), pp. 1265-1306.

Topel, Robert. 1984. "Equilibrium Earnings, Turnover and Unemployment: New Evidence," *Journal of Labor Economics*, 2(4), pp. 500-522.

Topel, Robert. 1990. "Specific Capital and Unemployment: Measuring the Costs and Consequences of Job Loss," *Carnegie-Rochester Conference Series on Public Policy*, vol. 33, pp. 181-214.

Topel, Robert. 1991. "Specific Capital, Mobility, and Wages: Wages Rise with Job Seniority," *Journal of Political Economy*, 99(1), pp. 145-76.

Topel, Robert, and Ward, Michael. 1991. "Job Mobility and the Careers of Young Men," *Quarterly Journal of Economics*, 107(2), pp. 439-479.

Troske, Kenneth R. 1996. "The Dynamic Adjustment Process of Firm Entry and Exit in Manufacturing and Finance, Insurance, and Real Estate," *Journal of Law and Economics*, 39(2), pp. 705-735.

Vinokur, Amiram D., Price, Richard H., Caplan, Robert D., van Ryn, Michelle, and Curran, Joan. 1995. "The Jobs I Preventive Intervention for Unemployed Individuals: Short- and Long-

Term Effects on Reemployment and Mental Health." In L.R. Murphy, J.J. Hurrell, Jr., S.L. Sauter and G.P. Keita (Eds.), *Job Stress Interventions*, (pp. 125-138). Washington, DC: American Psychological Association.

Von Wachter, Till. "Responding to Long-Term Unemployment." Testimony before the Subcommittee on Income Security and Family Support of the Committee on Ways and Means, June 10th, 2010.

Von Wachter, Till M., Handwerker, Elizabeth Weber, and Hildreth, Andrew K.G. 2011. "Estimating the `True' Cost of Job Loss: Evidence using Matched Data from California 1991-2000," Working paper.

Von Wachter, Till, Song, Jae, and Manchester, Joyce. 2009. "Long-Term Earnings Losses due to Mass Layoffs During the 1982 Recession: An Analysis Using U.S. Administrative Data from 1974 to 2004," Working paper.

Welch, Finis. 1970. "Education in Production," *Journal of Political Economy*, 78(1), pp. 35-59.